Life without Fu

a story of love, faith, illness & Hope

Carl M. White

Austin Brothers
— PUBLISHING —
www.abpbooks.com

Life Without Fu: A story or love, faith, illness & hope
Carl M., White

Published by Austin Brothers Publishing, Fort Worth, Texas
www.abpbooks.com

Copyright 2022 by Carl M. Whitre

The copyright supports and encourages the right to free expression. The purpose is to encourage writers and artists to continue producing work that enriches our culture.

Scanning, uploading, and distribution of this book without permission by the publisher is theft of the author's intellectual property. To obtain permission to use material from the book (other than for review purposes) contact terry@abpbooks.com.

ISBN: 978-1-7375807-5-1

Printed in the United States of America
2022 -- First Edition

This book is dedicated to...

*Dr. Jennifer Eubanks and all the care givers at
Meridian Oncology Associates,*

*Donna Rollins and the others who helped
giving care at home,*

*Dr. Willie Greer and the
countless people who provided prayer
and caring support to my Fu, me, and my children.*

*Thank you for listening, for remaining calm, for showing
compassion, for patiently explaining, for being professional, for
being personal, for laughing with us, for having clear focus, for
just being there.*

You made a difference for us.

Chapters

Introduction	1
Faith	5
Love	9
A Beautiful Soul	15
Teacher	19
Terminal	23
Treatments	29
Happiness	33
Home	37
Blessings	43
Encouragement	49
Hope	55
Epilogue – Observations On Grief	61

Foreword

Grief, a noun defined by Merriam-Webster as a deep and poignant distress caused by or as if by bereavement. Grief is the expression of love you have for the person who has passed from this life to eternity. While dealing with grief over the death of his wife, Dr. Carl White wrote, "Life is carrying on as if nothing has happened, as if nothing has changed…But running from pain is not the answer. It has to be faced, but it is so hard. It hurts bad."

Through the telling of the love story of Mutt and Fu, Bro. Carl, as we called him, brought back many memories of my friendship with them through the years. He became my Pastor and friend, and she became my friend and sister. We had a special connection from the start! I spent many hours playing games at their house with them and the children. Frances (Fu) was a fierce competitor! She became my "big sister" and was my Maid of Honor as Bro. Carl conducted the marriage ceremony. Though years and living in different places separated us, our friendship remained strong.

I will never forget the morning I spoke to Frances after she received the diagnosis. Through tears and trying to offer encouragement, she was the one who encouraged me with her fighting spirit! I texted numerous times to let her know I was praying that God would heal her and give her courage in the fight. In this love story, Bro. Carl makes note several times of Fu's courage and character. It is in the times of adversity that our true character shows. Her faith and trust were in her Savior and Lord, which was the basis of her character and courage.

As I read this beautiful tribute to Fu by Mutt, I cried tears for my friend and the struggle of grief he was going through. This tribute is the therapy he needed, and it gives the reader a glimpse of the love they shared, a love ordained and blessed by God. We will all experience the pain of death, but it is through faith in Christ that we know we will see our loved ones again.

Frances and I had a song we would always sing when being silly! It was by Ray Stevens titled "The Pirate Song." The verse talked about singing and dancing. I know she is singing and dancing in worship of our Lord, and one day we will again sing and dance.

Dr. Beth M. Cline, Ed.D., NCSP

Introduction

Late on a Sunday, I head out for an afternoon walk. Two older women, one of them a recent widow, pass by the front of my house as they often do, twice a day, talking about whatever it is women who are neighbors and friends talk about. I wonder if she is still talking about her late husband.

A younger woman in our neighborhood jogs by the front of the house, her tightly pulled ponytail bouncing back and forth on her shoulders as she pushes through another run. Sometimes her teen daughter, or husband, or both, run.

I finish my stretches and head out for a brisk mile and a half walk in the retreating light of the day. Down the road, a man and his son are in the front yard, picking up a bucket of baseballs after a pitch and swing workout. The kid is young, but he has a bat and an arm. It brings back memories of being in the front yard with my oldest son.

Life is carrying on as if nothing has happened, as if nothing has changed.

I turn two corners till I face west. The sky is coming alive with a beautiful palette of colors, just waiting for the Master's brush to create a stunning sunset of pink and orange. I thank God for the vista. Sadness fills my heart. My wife would have loved this sky. I would have loved sharing it with her, but I can't. She is gone.

This book is about our love for one another and my experiences with her over ten months as a dreaded disease slowly took her from me. In the days that followed her passing, I found myself at home alone, suffering, and fighting the temptation to flee the house and go somewhere, anywhere, that is not filled with reminders of our life. But running from pain is not the answer. It has to be faced, but it is so hard. It hurts bad.

So, I did what I have always done whenever I struggled. I started to write. These chapters are the result of that effort. For me, it was blessed therapy, recalling how wonderful she was, how deep our love was, and how blessed our life had been. It felt good to write about it.

It also felt good to tell how courageous she was in the face of a horrible disease that took so much from her. I want people to know about this. She was my hero and my soulmate, and she deserves to be known. Also, I believe that sharing our stories is always beneficial. It can provide a path for healing and can provide a guide to health.

These chapters were first posted one at a time on Facebook and my blog at pastorcarlwhite.com. Many people asked me to put all of it in a book. So, I have.

The resulting pages are a large part of my heart and soul. They tell a love story, our love story, and the sad story of her passing from this life. If you look, though, there is something beyond a love story here. To me, these chapters are filled with hope, even when it is not self-evident. I added Scripture passages and quotes between each chapter that we found helpful to aid in this.

If these pages bless you, share them with someone else. The only profit I want from this book is knowing that someone was blessed. All proceeds will go to the Frances White Encouragement Scholarship at Blue Mountain College, a small liberal arts school in Northeast Mississippi, a school known for producing outstanding teachers.

She would have liked that.

Faith

Fu is a French word (spelled *fou*) translated as mad or crazy. It was the nickname of my wife, Frances. She was a teen when she got that nickname in the summer of 1972 during Vacation Bible School at our church. She and I were helping in a preschool class, and she would sing the song *Little Rabbit Foo Foo*, along with the appropriate hand motions, to the delight of a group of four-year-olds.

It was a beautiful thing to watch. I was in love with her. We were 16.

One of the adults in the room started calling her Foo Foo. I shortened it to Foo and changed the spelling to "Fu."

It stuck.

Mutt was the nickname she gave me, which was a shortened version of the nickname my father had given me when I was a small child. I had a fair complexion and dark black hair. When my father gave me a crew cut, he said it looked like someone had smeared smut on my head.

It stuck, too, only I changed the spelling from "Smut" to "Smutt." Then Fu shortened it to Mutt.

By our senior year in high school, we were known throughout the school, especially among our friends, as Mutt and Fu. Even our senior jerseys reflected it. They were white with red letters spelling out "Provine," a large number "74" on the front and back - our graduation year - with our nicknames across the bottom rear. Hers said, "Fu." Mine said, "Mutt." We were a pair, meant to be together, practically inseparable.

My Fu passed away May 1, 2021, after a ten-month battle with Glioblastoma Multiforme: brain cancer. My heart has been broken ever since. After all, what is a Mutt without his Fu? I'm still trying to figure this out.

I hope you never have to go through the experience of hearing words like Glioblastoma Multiforme applied to someone you love. We left the neurosurgeon's office in shock. She had to be back in two days to be admitted to the hospital for a brain biopsy – brain surgery. It was during the COVID-19 pandemic. I could not be with her in the hospital.

We held each other those two days. We wept. Being without each other was unthinkable, especially at this time, but we had no choice. This awful reality was washing over us like waves on the shore, a stormy shore from which we could hardly find shelter.

But there was shelter to be had, and we did find it. We had the shelter of our love. She was my soul mate. How many people can say they found their soulmate at age 16 and got to spend over 48 years together, 43 of them as husband and wife. We were blessed.

We also had the shelter of Christ. By profession, I am a minister. She was a middle school English teacher and then a congressional aid. But of far more importance, we were Christ-followers. By faith, we claimed the promise of eternal life in Him. We believed that God does work all things together for good, but this was hard. When I left her that Sunday afternoon at the University of Mississippi Medical Center, I could not comprehend the reality that this was the beginning of life without Fu.

7th grade English Teacher

C.S. Lewis, *A Grief Observed*

"God has not been trying an experiment on my faith or love in order to find out their quality. He knew it already. It was I who didn't."

Psalm 116:10

I kept my faith, even when I said, "I am greatly afflicted."

Hebrews 11:1, 6

*Now faith is the assurance of things hoped for, the conviction of things not seen.
And without faith it is impossible to please God, for whoever would approach him must believe that he exists
and that he rewards those who seek him.*

Love

As a young teen, I saw how my oldest brother and his beautiful girlfriend loved each other. I remember lying in my bed one night with the blanket of my low self-esteem covering me and wondering if I would ever find someone who would love me. I prayed to God I would.

A young teen girl with a drunken father was praying for her family at about the same time. She had watched him point a gun at her mother. One day he pointed the gun at her, and her mother had had enough! Fu's parents divorced, and her mother and young-teen daughter struggled to get by. They were always close, but they were more like best friends by the time I came into the picture.

Fu told me that at age 15, she prayed God would bring her a Christian guy who would love her, provide for her, and protect her. Later, she told me that when we met, I was the answer to her prayer. She claimed God picked me for her.

It is pretty amazing to be told you are the answer to a girl's prayers.

I always saw it a little differently. I felt like God told me I could marry any Christian girl I could find, as long as I could convince her to have me. She said God picked me for her. I said God allowed me to pick her. Go figure!

Fu and Mutt in College

I always thought our first meeting in the front lobby of Provine High School in Jackson, MS was a chance meet. I was walking to class when she came by with her friend Cheryl, who was also my friend from band. Cheryl introduced us. I found out years, I mean, many years later, that Fu had asked Cheryl to introduce us. She had noticed me and wanted to meet me.

What I thought was serendipity was actually Fu directing events toward what she knew she wanted. They were waiting for me to come around the corner that morning. She did things like this all our life together, and I loved her for it.

Though we attended the same church, we hung out with different people. I hadn't noticed her yet. Then, at a Campus Life/Youth for Christ meeting, I saw her sitting on the floor with some other girls. I chose a chair right behind them.

Three things I noticed about her. One, her hair was long - halfway down her back - auburn colored and had a shine and a softness to it that was almost irresistible. I wanted to reach out and touch her hair. Second, her natural beauty. She had the sweetest smile and captivating blue eyes, and nice curves. And third – I know this sounds odd – but I noticed her posture. She sat up straight, exuding confidence and strength. But there was a problem. She had a boyfriend. I had to wait.

Apparently, Richard was not the answer to her prayers. (Sorry Richard.) Toward the end of our tenth-grade year, she became available, and I made my move. I honestly believed that I was the one taking the initiative, but in reality, she had been working on this for a while.

Early June of 1972, we had our first official date to see *Dr. Zhivago* at the old *Lamar Theater* in downtown Jackson. I worked dipping ice cream at *Baskin Robbins* in Westland Plaza that summer. She came by nearly every Saturday when I worked a shift. I would stop by her house every time I got off work before going home.

In the summer of '72, she spent a week with her Grandmother, like she did every summer. It liked to have killed me. My family went on a vacation for a week. I missed her so much she was all I could think about. When we got home on a Saturday, I asked if I could use the car to go see her. My mother said yes.

I knocked on the door, and her mother answered. She invited me in and called out to Frances that I was there. I heard her feet hit the floor and run from her bedroom. She came into the living room and jumped into my arms. Wow! She missed me as much as I missed her.

We were Mutt and Fu, and we knew we were meant to be together.

Sometimes it seemed like we were walking through life in an incandescent glow. We were so comfortable with one another; it seemed natural as breathing. I likened it to a miracle, an act of God being gracious to us, to me.

Five years later, in the summer of 1977, we became husband and wife. Forty-three years later, I stood beside her bed with our three adult children and watched her leave this life. And I became a Mutt without a Fu.

C. S. Lewis. Mere Christianity

God created things which had free will. That means creatures which can go either wrong or right. Some people think they can imagine a creature which was free but had no possibility of going wrong; I cannot. If a thing is free to be good, it is also free to be bad. And free will is what has made evil possible. Why, then, did God give them free will? Because free will, though it makes evil possible, is also the only thing that makes possible any love or goodness or joy worth having.

Psalm 73:26

*My flesh and my heart may fail,
but God is the strength of my heart and my portion forever.*

1 John 4:18

There is no fear in love, but perfect love casts out fear.

August 20, 1977, our Wedding Day

A Beautiful Soul

Fu means crazy in French, and she was, in her special way. First, she was crazy about me. What can I say? I didn't deserve it, but she loved me and believed in me. She was God's grace, extended to me through our relationship. It made me a better man.

The truth is she was always the better person. She was compassionate, kind, smart, and determined. Her piety ran deep and was strong. She knew what she wanted in life and went for it. She didn't want riches or fame. That never interested her. She wanted to have a happy marriage to a Christian man. She wanted to be a mother. And she wanted me to think I was responsible for the blessedness of our life together.

It took me a long time to realize it, but that was not true. She was the secret behind the beauty of our life together because she was a beautiful soul. I have a master's degree and an earned doctorate. I would have never achieved these things apart from her. When we started, I could not spell anything and could hardly write a complete sentence. I've written hundreds of sermons and published over a hundred articles; I have written numerous short stories and a novel. None of that would have happened without her.

However, her calling in life was not to be my wife but to be the mother of our children. Now, of course, I had a role in that. She, however, was in the driver's seat. She was crazy about being a mom.

Fu was an only child, primarily raised by her mother and Grandmother. She had three much younger male first cousins, which she saw only a couple of times a year. That was her family, and she was the center of it.

My father and mother raised me, and I was the fourth of five children with nearly a dozen cousins. I was the center of nothing except when misbehaving. I had the experience of a house full of kids. She had the experience of being the one and only child, yet somehow, she knew what to do when it came to raising children. I didn't.

My idea of discipline was to holler and threaten the little rascals to get them to act right. It did not work very well.

She would come in, gently and quietly take over, and soon they would be little angels. It involved redirecting, pointing their attention toward something else, listening carefully, and loving them tenderly. I don't know how she knew to do that, but instinctively, she did. I watched in amazement.

The truth is I was hardly in the game, but she made me feel like I was in charge; but I never was, not really. Early on, I realized that the smartest thing I could do in our family life was to follow her lead.

She loved being a mom, and since I helped make that become a reality, she loved me for it. And I loved her for giving me three wonderful children; children made wonderful by her nurturing and direction. There was a lot of love.

We needed a lot of love. We had three children in less than four years. We liked to joke about 1984 as a year to forget.

Our third child was born, and three weeks later, we moved. The oldest was just out of diapers; the middle one and the baby were in diapers; we were in a new house, a new church, with new people to meet, and a new community to learn. Looking back on it, I don't know how we did it. Rather, I don't know how she did it.

I was out too many nights, leaving her to take care of all three by herself. I had to learn about the families of my congregation and the needs of those families. Which meant I was too often disengaged from what was going on with my own family. Fu, however, was fully engaged, not only with our children but also with me.

She made it possible for us to succeed.

When I reflect on those days, I remember a blessed life as we raised our children. It wasn't easy. We struggled at times to get by. But what made it so good was being with my children, and most of all, with my Fu.

Angelita Lim

"I saw that you were perfect and I loved you. Then I saw that you were not perfect and I loved you even more."

Proverbs 31:26-31

*She opens her mouth with wisdom,
and the teaching of kindness is on her tongue.
She looks well to the ways of her household,
and does not eat the bread of idleness.
Her children rise up and call her happy;
her husband too, and he praises her:
"Many women have done excellently,
But you surpass them all."
Charm is deceitful, and beauty is vain,
But a woman who fears the Lord is to be praised.*

Colossians 3:19

Husbands, love your wives and never treat them harshl

Teacher

Fu wanted to be a 7th grade English teacher, and I am telling you, *that* is crazy. When we made our last move, she took a job in one of the area's more difficult schools. You could argue that this was the only job offered to her, but I would tell you she accepted the assignment as if it was from God himself, which it probably was. She was good at it.

Now, she never received any special recognition from the administration. However, she received two recognitions that meant the world to her, both from students. In 2008 and in 2011 the most outstanding students of the year chose Frances as the most influential teacher in their lives. Those two certificates are framed and on the wall in our home office.

Her students always showed improvement, and every year she would connect on a deep, even spiritual level with a handful. The first few years after she retired, we would come across former students who would run up and hug her and tell her with breathless enthusiasm what they have been doing with their lives.

After those occasions, I could see the deep sense of satisfaction in her face, and I realized the eternal impact of her life and ministry on the children of others. I was so proud of her and did everything I could to encourage her. That is what a Mutt is supposed to do for his Fu.

This is not to say teaching was easy. That road was full of twists and potholes, some large enough to swallow you. On a few occasions, a student would threaten her. But those were the exceptions. Most of her students responded positively. She would tell them a bad thing would happen if they did not behave. What was that bad thing? They could not stay in her class. By mid-year, most of her students wanted to be in her class.

A few students stayed in contact through *Facebook* or email. After she passed, a few students reached out to me. One successful writer made a small donation to the Frances White Encouragement Scholarship Fund we established in Fu's memory at Blue Mountain College.

It became really hard when her favorite principal was removed, and the new principal did not provide, she felt, the same level of support. She told me she did not want to sign another contract that spring. I told her that was fine. We no longer needed the income. "Come home," I said, "take it easy and let me take care of you."

That lasted about eight months. Her being at home was driving both of us crazy. A long-time friend, now a U. S. Congressman, had offered her a job a few years earlier. He hired her, and she became a Special Assistant for Constituent Services for Congressman Gregg Harper, focusing primarily on the needs of veterans. When he retired from Congress, she went to work for his successor, Congressman Michael Guest. She loved this work and the people with whom she associated. We were able to save most of her salary for a future we dreamed of, a future that never came.

She was most crazy about being a grandmother during the later period of our life. We have six amazing grandchildren and, at one point, three grand puppies. They were the joy of her life. When she became a grandmother, she stopped coloring her hair and let it turn its natural white. I fell in love with her beautiful auburn hair as a teen. As a middle-aged adult, I fell in love with her beautiful, soft white hair.

I miss many things about her, like helping her get ready for class or providing pizza as a reward for her students on special occasions. I miss visiting her in the Congressional office and going to lunch together. But touching and smelling her hair, that's the thing I miss the most as a Mutt without Fu.

Alexandra K. Trenfor

"The best teachers are those who show you where to look but don't tell you what to see."

Aristotle

"Teaching is the highest form of understanding."

Robert Heinlein

"When one teaches, two learn."

Proverbs 22:6

Start children off on the way they should go, and even when they are old they will not turn from it.

Titus 2:7-8

In everything set them an example by doing what is good. In your teaching show integrity, seriousness and soundness of speech that cannot be condemned.

Terminal

In June of 2020, she complained about her right-hand feeling and acting crazy. Then, while playing the piano at a funeral I was conducting, her right hand would not work. A few nights later, she fell. The next day she went to see our physician. He ordered an MRI, but it was three weeks before the earliest available appointment.

Then she fell again. I talked to our doctor on the phone, and he ordered a CT scan for the next morning. Afterward, back in his office, he told us the scan showed something in her brain. He sent us back to the imaging center for an emergency MRI.

There was definitely something there, so he made a work-in appointment for the next day with the head of neurosurgery at the University of Mississippi Medical Center. On that Friday, we heard the words Glioblastoma Multiforme for the first time.

We knew from the very beginning the outcome. The neurosurgeon at the University Medical Center made it perfectly clear. This was a terminal disease.

Terminal.

That word hit like a sledgehammer. I held her right hand with my right hand while I put my left arm around her. She shook like a leaf. We were both in shock.

It was Stage IV. Do nothing, he said, and she would survive eight to twelve weeks. If successful surgery were possible and successful treatments done, maybe two years. No surgery, but successful treatments, maybe a year. There was no cure, but hopefully, we could buy some time.

The neurosurgeon did not recommend surgery. There were four tumors, three in the left hemisphere and one in the right. Two were insignificant but would grow. In his words, the other two were in an elegant part of the brain. They were in the left hemisphere motor belt, the section that controls muscle movement and feelings on the right side. This explained her falls and the trouble playing the piano with her right hand.

We might find a surgeon who would operate if we tried, but removing the tumors from the motor belt would have devastating results. Plus, she would not survive four surgeries. So, we accepted his recommendation. It proved to be a wise decision.

We met a man at the oncology clinic who had a large tumor in the left hemisphere motor belt a few months later. He found a surgeon who would operate. It left him totally paralyzed on the right side. He could not move at all without help. It was so sad. He died a few weeks later.

Paralysis did come to her right side, but it happened gradually over many months, not overnight. It gave us time to adjust and plan. We worked on these things together.

It is shocking to hear such dreaded words as Stage IV Glioblastoma Multiforme. Learning to live with it is another thing altogether. In the face of this terrible diagnosis, Fu showed what she was really made of – courage and character. She showed her amazing courage and strength of character at every stage of this horrible disease. She showed me the way with every choice, never complaining, accepting each new struggle and humiliation. And a disease like this will humble you.

Ready to fight!

That is not to say she never struggled. Even a Fu with true grit has fragile moments. That's where I came in. I would hold her, weep with her, and tell her how loved she was.

I vowed in my heart that I would do anything and everything I could possibly do for my Fu. I would be with her in all things, holding her hand, comforting her, encouraging her – I would not leave her side. As my Fu, she was with me in all things; she held my hand, comforted me, encouraged me, and stayed by my side - for as long as she could.

She showed that grit time and again as the disease progressed. One particularly difficult moment was when I had to shave her head. The type of chemo she received did not cause her hair to fall out. However, her doctors prescribed a treatment that consisted of placing magnetic fields on her head to try and suppress the growth of the tumors. In clinical trials, it had shown some success. This necessitated the shave. She wanted me to do it, not her hairdresser. So, I did.

We both cried.

I have locks of her beautiful white hair in a plastic bag in my sock drawer. Isn't it crazy? I don't know what to do with them, but I can never throw them away. It's just a tiny, very personal, physical part of her that I get to keep as I try to figure out life without Fu.

C. S. Lewis, *The Problem with Pain*

"Try to exclude the possibility of suffering which the order of nature and the existence of free-wills involve, and you find that you have excluded life itself."

Psalm 119:50

*My comfort in my suffering is this:
Your promise preserves my life.*

Matthew 11:28

*Come to me, all you who are weary and burdened,
and I will give you rest.*

Ready for church two weeks after glioblastoma multiforme diagnosis.

Treatments

A few days after coming home from the brain biopsy, the tumors showed themselves. She had taken a shower – the last one she would take without my help – and was sitting on a stool in front of the bathroom mirror, brushing her beautiful white hair when it happened.

She called to me. "Mutt! Something is not right," she said. "Something is happening."

Then she began to shake on her right side. I rushed to her and held her up on the stool as the shaking increased. It stayed on the right side, but it was powerful and uncontrollable, lasting several minutes, minutes that seemed like forever. I continued to hold her on the stool as she wept. I wept with her. It left us both shaken and afraid.

After a couple of uneventful days since coming home, the tumors decided to remind us that they were still there and could do whatever they pleased. Our doctor started her on anti-seizure medication that day.

The next day, sitting on the couch, she had another seizure. It was not as strong but lasted longer than the first one. After it was over, I could see the resolve in her eyes. Her eyes were saying, "I know what this is now. I can handle this."

The first big decision was not to pursue the surgical option. The second big decision was she would not take this lying down. She would fight!

Thus began this tug of war with the tumors. My Fu fought them at every turn. Even so, she lost one ability after another. The doctors added one drug after another to try and control or lessen the symptoms, but there were difficult side effects. It was a losing battle, but Fu would never admit it.

We went from walking with a walker as a precaution in July to needing a walker to walk in August; to using a wheelchair and the walker in September; to being wheelchair-bound with the walker used for transfers in October, November, and December; to a wheelchair and needing extra physical help to make transfers into the new year; to being bed bound near the end.

She grew more and more dependent on help. Every motion, every movement, everything grew harder. Her energy level ran low faster. She slept a little more each passing week. She lost language abilities, searching for words that she knew. Her world became smaller and smaller. Even her eyesight grew dim.

But my Fu, she never gave up! She stayed positive, asking me on many mornings, "who can I encourage today?" The growing paralyzes on her right side meant she could no longer type or write. So, I would write notes for her to be mailed, type emails for her to be sent, and help her make phone calls. Visitors came to lift her spirits, but she surprised them by lifting their spirits. I marveled at her faith and courage.

The third big decision was to embark on an aggressive treatment regimen, starting with radiation and leading to powerful chemotherapy. The radiation was perhaps the hardest challenge of all.

She was claustrophobic. To have radiation treatments for brain tumors meant she would be strapped to a table with a mesh mask on her face that was also attached to the table. She could not move at all. Then the entire table slid into a tunnel where the machine spun around her, radiating her head and hopefully shrinking the tumors. The treatment didn't last very long, but that didn't matter. She could not do it without a pill. We called it her "or else pill." She had better take it 30 minutes before beginning treatments, or else!

At the same time, she took a chemo pill every night. Later she received chemo infusions every two weeks and five pills once a month. Miraculously, she got nauseated only once; but the chemo, along with the radiation, zapped her strength. They also depleted her blood counts, resulting in brief hospital stays, trips to get platelets and blood, and seemingly endless trips to have lab work.

I tried as hard as I could to care for her with compassion and tenderness. I vowed to myself to speak only kind and loving words to her. And if she needed something or wanted to go somewhere – her wish was my command.

Our children and grandchildren were there as much as they could be, but this was the age of Covid-19. Our Thanksgiving plans were canceled because of it. As a result, we spent Thanksgiving 2020 alone.

I had known for years that it is the nature of human relationships that they end in pain. It may be the pain of relational abuse or neglect. It may be the pain of abandonment or rejection. Often it is the pain of death.

Hard as I worked, there were constant reminders that this was how it was going to end. Pray as I may, nothing was going to change the trajectory. I was on the path toward a life without Fu.

C. S. Lewis, *The Problem with Pain*

"...it is natural for us to wish that God had designed for us a less glorious and less arduous destiny; but then we are wishing not for more love but for less."

Psalm 41:3

*The Lord sustains them on their sickbed;
in their illness you heal all their infirmities.*

1 Corinthians 12: 30-31, 13:1, 13

*Do all possess gifts of healing? Do all speak in tongues?
Do all interpret? But strive for the greater gifts.
And I will show you a still more excellent way.*

*If I speak in the tongues of mortals and of angels,
but do not have love, I am a noisy gong or a clanging cymbal.*

*And now, faith, hope, and love abide, these three;
and the greatest of these is love.*

Happiness

We were Mutt and Fu, Fu and Mutt. Our love was deep and profound, and I believe to this day, special. What was the secret to our happiness together? Fu! She was an amazing person and a truly beautiful soul. I've thought about what made her this way and came to a few conclusions.

First, she was determined. When she knew what she wanted, she went for it. She went all out for it, and she did not easily give up. If one approach didn't work out, she would try another.

Now, if it didn't work out, she chalked it up as a learning experience. Everything was a potential learning experience. She never let an event pass without seeking to learn or to teach her children and me.

Second, she was competitive, a streak that came out when playing games. If I played a game with one of our children, I usually let them win, not so with Fu. If a child beat her in a game, it was because they beat her. She didn't believe in allowing a child to win just because they were a child. Now, she was really careful to make sure the game was appropriate to the child, but she wanted them to do well and do it on their own. So, after a game they lost, she would talk to them about why they lost. Everything was a potential learning experience in her mind. Nothing was a waste in her view of life.

Third, she liked to win. She liked winning so much she would not play a game she couldn't win. We had a ping pong table as our children entered their teen years. She would play with them but not with me. I would easily beat her, so she just wouldn't play me.

Sometimes I would beg her to play. Then the bargaining began. I had to promise no slams, no spins on the ball, and to only hit the ball to her so that she could return it. Those were the terms. As I said, she liked to win.

I just liked to play. Winning and losing was never a big deal to me at first. But after many years of only playing games she could win and being consistently on the losing side, I grew resentful. I regret that.

Fourth, she took a mature view of things. We were intensely in love as teens, but to uphold Christian virtue meant we could only be so close. I started pushing her too much during our senior year. So, she broke up with me a month before our senior prom, taking the mature view.

Things happen on prom night, you know.

She told me I needed to grow up. However, she did not tell me her plan, which was to give us a little time apart to cool things down before coming back together for the sprint to marriage.

I was devastated. The Sunday morning after our breakup, I was at her house early to take her to church, as usual. Another guy was there to get her! I'm sure she considered it a learning experience, but I did not like what I was learning.

She started dating that guy who was already a student at Mississippi College, where Fu and I planned to attend that fall. I could not stand the thought of seeing her on campus with someone else, so at the last minute, I submitted an application to the University of Southern Mississippi and headed south.

We could not be around each other as friends, but we could write letters to each other, sharing our deepest thoughts. Over the next two years, two or three letters a week flew between USM and MC.

I have a treasure. I have all of these letters. Someday, when I feel up to it, I will pull them out and start pairing them; what she wrote, what I wrote in response, and vice versa.

After only a few weeks, she broke up with that other guy, but she didn't tell me until just before Christmas break. I went home that Friday and was at her house that evening. It was the first time I had been alone with her in months.

Fu gave me the ground rules. We could date again, some, but we were both free to date other people. That was fine with me, just as long as I had a fighting chance with her.

She had many dates in the second half of our freshman year and our sophomore year in college. I never had another date with anyone else. There was no one else. At the end of our sophomore year, I convinced her to leave MC and join me that fall at USM.

I had her back. I think I was more mature. Her plan, as usual, worked, and we were Mutt and Fu again.

Denis Waitley

Happiness cannot be traveled to, owned, earned, worn or consumed. Happiness is the spiritual experience of living every minute with love, grace, and gratitude.

Psalm 40:4

Happy *are those who make the Lord their trust, who do not turn to the proud…*

John 16:22

So you have pain now; but I will see you again, and your hearts will rejoice, and no one will take your joy from you.

Home

In college, I believed God was calling me to the pastorate. Frances told me then that since junior high school, she had felt called to be a pastor's wife. She was always a step or two ahead of me. Thus, when it came to my career path, she was ready to go with me anywhere, even to Louisville, Kentucky. We loaded up a small U-Haul in August of 1978 and headed for seminary. I took her away from home.

That meant leaving her mother, Bobbye. This was very hard for Fu. They had been through so much together and were extraordinarily close. Unfortunately, as the next three years unfolded, it got much harder.

In January of 1980 came the news we were expecting our first child. She was so excited. I was so uncertain. Natural childbirth was the new thing, so we signed up for a Lamaze class and started preparing for the coming of our son. Those classes scared me to death. I tried to hide that from her, but she saw right through me. I didn't know how we were going to pay for it all. She would smile at me and say, "It will all work out."

Of course, we didn't know it was a boy. This was before the days of detailed sonograms. But we did know the baby was due in late September. She and her mother were ecstatic. Bobbye planned to visit early that summer and then be back in the fall for the birth.

Leaving for seminary in Louisville, KY, summer of 1978

The summer of 1980 was one of the hottest on record in Louisville, KY. Pregnant and growing, Fu could not get cool. We bought a small air conditioner on credit from Sears and put it in the window of the main room of our unairconditioned, 1920s era, third-floor apartment. By August, I moved the mattress off our bed and onto the living room floor so the air could blow directly on her. She was still hot!

Bobbye did not get to visit us early that summer. She was having health issues. Two weeks before the due date, she was admitted to the hospital, and they discovered she had ovarian cancer. In surgery, they opened her up and, after an examination, closed her back. The Doctor said if the chemo didn't help, she might not live another two months.

Fu was panic-stricken. We asked her Doctor about traveling to Mississippi. He said no. We asked him to induce labor early. He said no. We had to wait. Our boy didn't help in the matter, either. He came two days late.

David was born at Baptist East, the newest hospital at the time in Louisville, Kentucky. She went into labor on a Saturday afternoon. Our closest friends, Stephen and Karen, went with us to the hospital, but they had to leave early to travel to a weekend pastorate.

The only time I can remember Fu cursing at me was during labor. I tried to coach her to breathe as we were taught in the birthing classes. She looked at me and said, "Just shut the hell up!"

I backed away in shock. I couldn't believe that came from her mouth. The nurse suggested I step out into the waiting room and get a sip of water. The waiting room was packed full of people. I looked around the room.

There were expectant fathers, nervously laughing. There were expectant grandparents, happy and excited. There were even a few children in the room. They looked bored because they had to be there and were not excited about the intrusion coming into their lives. But they were there, waiting for the miracle of new life. They were there as a family to support the mother-to-be who was doing all the work in the labor unit.

Fu and I were alone. There was no one in the waiting room for us. It's not that we lacked friends. We were seminary students. It was a Saturday night, and our friends were gone to weekend churches. People surrounded us, but we were by ourselves. Her mother was supposed to be there with her, but Bobbye was in the hospital in Jackson. Her Grandmother was in Jackson helping Bobbye. My mother was coming to help but would not be there for another day.

I went back to Fu's bedside. I didn't tell her anything about the waiting room. I dialed back the Lamaze coaching a bit, and we focused on the work to be done together.

We celebrated the birth of our first child, David, just the two of us, along with a few kind nurses. Thankfully, he was healthy and strong. There was unbelievable joy, and at the same time, tears of sadness because her mother was not able to be there.

All the other women had used painkillers in the recovery room, and they were out cold. Frances had given birth all-natural. (She would do that two more times.) Since the nursery was full, they allowed David to stay with us in recovery for hours. She began to nurse him. A kind-hearted attendant ran a phone to her bed, and we called her mother's hospital room. David cried on the phone for Bobbye. I think Fu pinched him.

There we were, Mutt and Fu with little baby David, just the three of us. I had a realization that night that helped us through the itinerant life of a ministerial family. Home was wherever we were together. That night home was in the recovery room of Baptist East Hospital in Louisville, KY. We were together. We were home.

We went back to our apartment soon with little David. My mother arrived to help for a few days. Our friends were all there to offer support. Then, when David was nine days old, I put him and his mother on a plane to Mississippi.

By God's grace, Fu's mother lived for two more years. She got to see us move back to Mississippi and hold her first grandson. Fu got to spend precious time with her mother. It meant that she would be in Jackson with our son while I remained in the Delta, pastoring our little church, but it was ok. I knew she was where she needed to be. I also knew she would be back with me and that we would be home again.

Now I'm trying to figure out what home is without Fu.

Laura Ingalls Wilder

Home is the nicest word there is.

Psalm 127:1

Unless the Lord builds the house, those who build it labor in vain.

John 14:23

Jesus answered him, "Those who love me will keep my word, and my Father will love them, and we will come to them and make our home with them."

A proud mom, cir. 1984

Blessings

I didn't realize it at the time, but Fu trained me to take care of her one day.

Having lost her mother early, her Grandmother, Frances Dodds, was pretty much her family, besides the kids and me. We visited her often. She visited and stayed with us even more often.

In 2000, when we made our final move, we had a great blessing – Fu's Grandmother came to live with us. At first, she took care of us; washing clothes, cleaning the house, having dinner ready when we would get home. It was delightful watching her enjoy our three children, who, every evening, entertained her with their teenage experiences. Then, as time went by, Fu increasingly took care of her.

She was known as Grandmother to all who knew her. When she had her first stroke, we almost lost her. After a stay in the hospital, she came back to the house, and we hired a day sitter to be with her Monday through Friday. Nights and weekends, Fu took care of her, a task that grew more and more intense.

After Grandmother's second stroke, she went briefly to a nursing home and later an assisted living facility. We kept the day sitter, a loyal and loving woman named Shirley, but Fu would be over there every evening, seven days a week, with her Grandmother and helping her get to bed.

Grandmother lived to be over 100 years old. Fu's faith that God was in control and her determination to help her Grandmother never wavered. As her Mutt, I never wavered in my support of Fu. I knew a day would come in God's timing when it would just be us. I could wait on the Lord. I had no inkling that the example of her commitment and passion in taking care of her Grandmother was a training ground for me.

Taking care of Fu was a labor of love. As her illness progressed, we established a routine, but things got harder. Still, we had some great days. We even had a lot of fun.

One of the blessings during these days was Donna, a retired nurse who came to help us. Fu did not think we needed extra help. I prayed for help and asked God to show me how to handle the coming days and weeks. Willie Greer, a very good friend and a retired doctor, came weekly to check on us. He called one night and said he was bringing someone over for us to meet on Sunday afternoon. That is how we met Donna.

We all sat together in the den, exchanging small talk. I suddenly realized this was a job interview. Dr. Greer's sweet wife had passed away about two years earlier, and Donna had helped them. They knew each other from many years working together at one of the area hospitals.

The good Doctor stood up, signaling that they were ready to leave. He said Donna could be here Monday morning at about 8:30. They left, and that is how Donna was hired. She quickly became so much more. She was a blessed part of our family.

Idleness was never a part of Donna's life. She threw herself at helping us, from cooking, cleaning the house, doing laundry, and helping me with the personal tasks of taking care of Fu. I had found my own way to do certain things. She showed me better ways to do everything.

At first, Fu did not like having a person in the house nearly every day. But Donna's sweet, Christ-like spirit and servant's heart quickly won Fu over. Our children and grandchildren came to love Donna.

Our middle son, Dan, a college professor, was visiting one day. I needed to run some errands, so I left Fu in Dan and Donna's care. I had put a bird feeder out near the patio so Fu could see the birds. We also put corn feed out in the yard, attracting seven or eight deer at times. Fu could sit for hours, wide-eyed, as she scanned the feeder and the yard for signs of life.

But the squirrels were a nuisance. Like Olympic acrobatics, they found ways to steal the food from the bird feeder. She wanted me to do something about the squirrels, but I didn't know what to do.

I returned from my errands that day and carried a large bag of corn feed to the backyard. When I came around the corner of the house, I could not believe what I saw.

To my utter surprise, there was Fu in her wheelchair, wrapped in blankets and wearing Dan's coat with the hood up, sitting in her greenhouse with a BB gun across her lap. She was laughing so hard I thought she would drop the gun. Dan was there too, laughing with her.

Fu asked Dan and Donna to help her get rid of the squirrels, so they came up with a plan. They rolled her outside and positioned her in the greenhouse with my BB gun. It was a cold, February morning squirrel hunt, and I messed it up walking around the corner of the house, chasing the squirrels off.

Of course, Fu could not have shot that gun. By this point, her right arm was practically useless. Trying to keep things light, I gave that arm a nickname. We called it Floppy, and it caught on. Donna, our kids, and grandkids referred to that right arm as Floppy.

One day our eldest son, David, a pastor, was there. He was sitting next to his mother, on her right side, talking. He said something she didn't like, so she picked up her right arm with her left hand and threw it at him, hitting him.

It became a thing. We laughed and laughed about it, telling visitors to be careful what they said because if Fu didn't like it, she would hit them with Floppy.

Fu and Dan in the greenhouse

Floppy even had its own pillow. Each night as we settled into bed, I used a special pillow to prop Floppy up to help with circulation. Sometimes I would forget. She would hold up and shake Floppy, threatening me if I didn't get Floppy's pillow over there swiftly.

When all three children, spouses, and all six grandchildren and grand puppies were there, laughter flowed like sweet honey throughout the house. Fu would be right in the middle of it, smiling, basking in the warmth of her family. She loved playing card games, but she lost the ability to handle cards, so a grandchild would be her helper. She mostly watched her family play, enjoying every minute of it.

    Like the calm before the storm, those days of blessings allowed us, for just a little while, to forget where this was headed. In the end, my grandchildren would lose their Grandmother, my children would lose their mother, and I would lose my wife and become a Mutt without a Fu.

John Calvin

However many blessings we expect from God, His infinite liberality will always exceed all our wishes and our thoughts.

Psalm 144:15

Happy are the people to whom such blessings fall; happy are the people whose God is the Lord.

Ephesians 1:3

Blessed be the God and Father of our Lord Jesus Christ, who has blessed us in Christ with every spiritual blessing in the heavenly places,

Encouragement

Frances was bedridden. We came home after nearly two weeks in the hospital in late April to hospice care. Her Doctor tried to get her into a swing bed. The hope was that with intense physical therapy, she would get strong enough to have more chemo treatments. It had been over a month since the last one.

Her oncologist came into her room and sat on the bed next to her. She tried, the doctor said, but all four rehabs turned us down. "You have to show the possibility of improvement to be accepted," she told Frances, gently.

I looked at Fu. She was angry. She was hurt. Fu looked at me with tears and said with broken language, "there's nothing to slow down the tumors."

After a few moments, she asked what was next. The Doctor said home and hospice.

We looked intensely at one another like we had done countless times.

Over the years, one of my favorite moments of each day was when we went to bed. Before turning out the lights, we turned toward one another, our noses almost touching, and looked deeply into each other's eyes. Usually, nothing needed to be said. Sometimes I would tell her how much I loved her or how pretty she was.

Often, we played this little game she came up with early in our marriage. She used it to help me identify my feelings and express them. The rules were simple: at any time, one of us could ask the other, "Who are you?" You had to answer who you were at that moment. One day she would be a tired mom and schoolteacher, or I would be a frustrated pastor. Other times we would be some other version of ourselves, but you had to answer.

This little game helped us get to know each other on a deeper level. And for me, someone who had trouble even identifying feelings, it was therapeutic.

Most of the time, while looking each other deep in the eyes, we would simply smile at each other. We were Mutt and Fu, and we were together. We were home. Then, she would turn out the light and be asleep in moments while I read or watched TV.

We looked at one another in the hospital room like we had done for years. It didn't need to be said. We understood it instinctively. Who was she? She was my love, who was dying of brain cancer. Who was I? I was a broken-hearted man. The reality of it all washed over us in waves and waves of sadness.

Dr. Jennifer Eubanks, Fu's oncologist, helped us fight this terrible disease for ten months. She was wonderfully attentive, listened carefully, and treated us with great compassion. She never failed to respond when we had questions or needed help.

Dr. Eubanks and I went out into the hall to talk. Through the door, Fu could see us. Afterward, I could tell she was angry at me, but I didn't understand why. Later, after Fu was home, our daughter told me why. She was angry because Dr. Eubanks and I talked about her away from her presence.

That was true, but I felt I needed to have a hard conversation about how things were unfolding. I didn't think about it until much later, but from her perspective, I was starting to make decisions without her, like a Mutt without a Fu.

Our daughter Katie, a schoolteacher and pastor's wife, came each weekend she was able to help, but mostly to be with her mother. The last weekend in the hospital, Katie relieved me, and I got to go home for the night. Late that night, Katie went out into the hall to the nurse's station to get her mother some fruit juice. This was still during the pandemic, and she forgot to put on her mask. A nurse saw her from down the hall and yelled at her. If she didn't put on her mask, she would be kicked out of the hospital!

Katie scurried back to the room and told her mother about the mask police in the hall. Katie heard a growling noise. It was Fu. She showed her displeasure at that nurse and her support for her baby girl by growling like a mother bear protecting her cub. A little later, Fu told Katie, with broken language, that they should hide and, when the nurse came in, jump out and growl at her.

She still had her sense of humor.

A few days later, an ambulance brought her to the house. Once home, she never got out of bed again. The hospice nurse came, the hospice social worker came, and the hospice care assistant came. Then a friend of mine, the hospice chaplain, came.

He and his wife had been dreadfully ill with Covid-19 earlier in the year, and she was currently in the hospital with respiratory problems. After talking to Fu for a few moments, he offered to pray for us. He held Frances' hand and prayed a sweet prayer. After the amen, Fu would not let go of his hand. Instead, she started praying out loud for him and his wife.

Because of the tumors, she would start a sentence but could not find the right words to finish it. She would start a prayer thought, get stuck searching for the words, and then say, "Lord you know." She did that several times. Then she said, "Amen."

I walked my friend out through our garage. He stopped. Through tears, the chaplain said that in all his years of doing hospice chaplaincy work, that had never happened before. Never had a client prayed for him or his wife.

That was my Fu, still wanting to encourage someone.

She would survive nine days on hospice care.

Our three children were doing their best to be there. Each day she was weaker and less alert. The Hospice nurse came by and spent a few minutes examining her. Then, she and Donna talked. I approached to learn what they were saying.

The nurse turned to me and asked when all three of our children would be home again.

"Not until Sunday afternoon," I told her.

She said, "That's not soon enough."

I was shocked! I backed up till I hit the kitchen counter. I felt faint. This was Wednesday. Though I had known from the beginning the ultimate outcome, I couldn't believe it was coming on so fast.

That night I wept alone as I confronted the reality of life without Fu.

Zig Ziglar

When you encourage others, you in the process are encouraged because you're making a commitment and difference in that person's life. Encouragement really does make a difference.

Romans 15:4

For whatever was written in former days was written for our instruction, so that by steadfastness and by the encouragement of the scriptures we might have hope.

Isaiah 40:31

Those who wait for the Lord shall renew their strength, they shall mount up with wings like eagles, they shall run and not be weary, they shall walk and not faint.

Hope

We had been praying for several specific things. One, that she would not be in much pain. Only in the last few days did we need to start using pain meds. Two, that she would not linger unaware for a long time. She had been sleeping a lot, but only since starting the pain meds had she been completely unaware.

Third, we prayed that I would stay healthy to see this all the way through. Three years earlier, I was diagnosed with non-Hodgkin lymphoma. I was now considered in remission. I also had some serious heart issues. Two weeks after she died, I had a heart attack and had three stents. But I stayed healthy long enough to care for her to the end.

Fourth, since coming home to hospice care, we prayed that she would not die on our oldest granddaughter's birthday, which was May 2. Our three children and I were standing around her bed as she took her last breath in the early morning hours of May 1.

I've come to understand that this is how God works. We love to hear stories about how God answers big prayers in big ways. I now see that He most often answers prayers in small ways, small things that alone may not seem that significant but, when taken together, are breath-taking. He was with us for the entire journey, and we were, every day, under His providential care.

That is how it was with my Fu and the ten months of her terrible illness. Oh, I prayed nearly every night that she would be healed, but I also prayed that both of us would get the rest we needed, which He granted. I prayed for insight so I could respond to her needs, which He did. I prayed for help, and He sent Donna. I prayed for the peace that passes understanding, and He granted that to both of us.

That's not to say we avoided the "why" questions or the mental anguish and anger associated with such an illness. But God was gracious, giving us the strength to not linger there. Our faith was strong because both of us had trusted Christ in our youth and had invested time in spiritual formation. Instead of expending energy wallowing in self-pity and anger, our faith in Christ allowed us to acknowledge the reality of the pain but rise above it, to encourage others, and enjoy nearly every minute we had.

I don't know how anyone could face something like this without faith.

Now that she is gone, I am praying for patience and help to see a new future, one without my Fu. How's it going, you ask?

It's a mixed bag. On the one hand, due to the heart issues, I've been to cardio rehab, and I've worked on changing my lifestyle. Pounds I long needed to lose have fallen off. I feel better physically than I have in years.

On the other hand, waves of sadness still overwhelm me unexpectedly. Small reminders of her can catch me off guard - a whiff of her cologne or a glimpse of a woman with white hair like hers.

Some days I just don't want to get up. Thus far, I have been able to push through that to do what I need to do. I've realized that idleness is my worst enemy, so I try to stay busy. Also, too much alone time leads to self-pity, which is not good for anyone. However, I do allow myself an occasional pity party. I figured I've earned it.

Some people say there are no tears in heaven. That makes no sense to me. There must be tears in heaven. If there are no tears, how could He wipe away our tears? In heaven, the Lord himself comforts us.

In my heart, I see her looking at me, tears in her eyes, but with that smile where the ends of her mouth actually turn down, like she knows something, something I can't know, something too wonderful for words. Like she knows in the end everything is going to be ok. That's when I am comforted.

It also helps to talk to her, at least "the her" I know in my heart. I sit on the edge of our bed, looking at beautiful photos of her, of us. I kiss the tip of my finger and touch it to her lips in a photo wishing it was really her as if wishing can make it come true.

I talk about her to my family, my friends, or pretty much anyone, without apology. Many mornings I look at her picture and say, "Good morning, my love." Many evenings I tell her good night. And once a month, I try to visit her grave.

She is buried three hours north of our home, next to her mother and Grandmother. As of this writing, it has only been six months. It is still hard to visit the gravesite and then hard to leave. But I have to go. I need to talk to her there. I imagine this need to visit the grave will fade in time, but it hasn't yet.

I know she is not there. I have no illusions about the finality of death in this life. The separation is real and profound. My conversations are not with her disembodied spirit, but with the memory I have of her in my heart. Here's the ironic thing about this memory: I control it. I can remember however I choose. In memory, I'm able to bend her to my will, something I could never do in life. And I will, in time, release more and more of her memory. This is called the grief process.

As a pastor for over 40 years, I observed a lot of grief. My advice to people is to face it one day at a time. Don't self-medicate or try to run from it. Don't try to replace your losses too fast. God created us as grieving creatures. He means for us to walk through grief, not to avoid it or go around it. After all, grief is an expression of love.

I also tell people, don't waste your grief. By that, I mean there is spiritual growth here that you may not find anywhere else. Seek the Lord earnestly. Read Holy Scriptures and pray regularly and honestly. Tell God how you really feel. He can handle your questions and your anger. He can comfort your broken heart. He has comforted mine.

Find people of faith who are themselves going through grief and share with them and allow them to share with you. Listen with ears of faith, and the Holy Spirit will teach you.

I also advise people not to make major life changes until they get through that year of firsts; first birthday, first anniversary, first holidays, etc. These days are harder than I ever imagined. I don't want to linger here. I want this to be over. I want to run away.

I'm trying to take my own advice.

In the days immediately following her death, my head was in a fog. Some days the fog returns, but I'm now beginning to see a future. I'm not at peace with it yet, but I am confident that peace will come

More than ever, Isaiah 40:31 speaks to me:

Yet those who wait for the Lord will gain new strength;
They will mount up with wings like eagles,

They will run and not get tired,
They will walk and not become weary.

Some days it is hard to walk. On those days, He keeps me from being too weary. On other days things are so busy I have to run to keep up. He won't let me get too tired.

And one day, I am certain, with wings of faith, I will soar again.

I have gratitude in my heart for my Fu and the wonderful years we had together. That gratitude gives me strength. I'm too blessed to be forever stressed. Yes, I am a Mutt without my Fu, but I got to be with her for nearly 50 years. We will be together again in His timing, according to His will. I can wait for the Lord.

It's a learning experience, life without Fu.

Thanksgiving 2021

Epilogue – Observations On Grief

I've spent a lifetime observing grief, but never before have I confronted grief head-on. I claim no expertise on the subject. There are many resources available to provide help and guidance. However, I would like to offer a few observations from a fellow grief traveler.

Grief is not neat and orderly. It is not confined to a specific timetable. It can't be walked through in seven easy steps. Rather, grief comes – at least in my experience – in waves, some powerful enough to knock you down, others more subtle and soft, but it comes.

It comes unexpectedly. Sometimes the smallest happening can trigger sadness: a smell, an item at the grocery store, the innocent word of a friend. At other times you know exactly what will happen when you walk into a room or begin a conversation.

I thought that I would be smarter than grief because of my education and pastoral experience. I've learned that the emotions of grief cannot be outsmarted. They slip into my conscious life in surprising and unexpected ways, especially when I am tired or idle.

I have lost grandparents, aunts, and uncles, but these loved relatives were rather distant. When Frances' mother died, that was close at hand, but my focus was on my wife and her loss. I lost both of my parents, but they had reached a point of declining health where, as my Dad said, "Son, this is not living." Death came as a friend.

The loss of my wife was different: up-close, personal. From my perspective, hers was an unfinished life. A loss like this brings a kind of pain, which I have never known before. The natural reaction is to try and escape the pain. It hurts so bad, but you cannot avoid it, nor can you rush it. As the commercial says, a good wine takes time. So does good grief.

Good grief is not a catchphrase like Charlie Brown uses in Peanuts. Nor is it an oxymoron, though it would seem that these two words – good and grief - simply do not belong together. But they do, at least for those who walk by faith in Christ. I can only speak about grief in terms of my faith because faith informs every aspect of my life. Faith brings hope. Walking by faith can make the words "good" and "grief" come together in a meaningful way. But it is not easy.

Losing someone you deeply love, whether a spouse, a parent, or a child, rips the fabric of the soul. I once did a funeral service with a Jewish Rabbi. (It's a long story.) He stood at the pulpit of my Baptist church with a small piece of black cloth. Before all the family and friends, he made a tear in it and then made this observation: the tear in the cloth will never go away.

A skilled seamstress can mend it, but the tear in the cloth is still there, under the mend. It will always be there.

I've thought about what he said over the years. Time will deaden the pain. Life goes on, and I will, eventually, move on with it. But this tear in the fabric of my soul will still be there. But will it always be there?

My faith tells me this: *"For God so loved the world that he gave his only Son, so that everyone who believes in him may not perish but may have eternal life."* (John 3:16) Did you notice these words: "believe," "not perish," and "eternal life?" This means that all of life has purpose in Him, and because of the one resurrected from the grave, death is changed to mean something different. Instead of an ending, it means a passage - passing from one life to another life. My sweet Fu passed to a new life, so will I, and so can you. This faith in Jesus Christ brings the hope that ultimately can heal the torn fabric of your soul.

Maybe to you, this sounds like cheap religious platitudes. I understand that, but it is not. For me, it is real, tangible hope. The Apostle John also writes: *"But to all who received him, who believed in his name, he gave power to become children of God, who were born, not of blood or of the will of the flesh or of the will of man, but of God."* (John 1:12-13)

What a magnificent yet mysterious thought, being born of God. That is the audacious claim of the Christian faith. My Frances was born of God. I believe I have been, too. My grief is still messy and unexpectedly painful, but I have hope. There is a lot I still have to learn about the experience, but I see peace in my future. I see my Lord waiting for me, and my Fu is there with Him. My wish for you is to find that same hope in Christ.

CPSIA information can be obtained
at www.ICGtesting.com
Printed in the USA
LVHW081349290322
714698LV00009B/335